MW00512572

To the only God, our Savior,
through Jesus Christ our Lord,
be glory, majesty, dominion, and
authority, before all time and
now and forever. Amen.

JUDE 1:25

Celebrate Salvation!®

Saved!
Rescued by Grace

Stage A - Foundational Principles of the Good News

The Joy of Christian Discipleship Series
Book 1

Dr. Bill Morehouse

His Kingdom Press

About Dr. Bill Morehouse

Dr. Morehouse was raised in a traditional Christian home in the 1950's and functionally became a humanist during college and medical school in the 1960's. After completing his medical residency in Family Medicine in the early 1970's he embarked on a career of serving the poor but soon found that his secular faith and alternative lifestyle were woefully inadequate to the task.

In 1974 he underwent a dramatic conversion from the philosophy and lifestyle he had been living to a wholehearted commitment to Jesus as his LORD and Savior. After returning to medicine and marrying in 1975, he and his wife dedicated themselves to growing in faith, raising their family of four children (plus spouses and grandchildren), and providing Christ-centered service to some of the most disadvantaged members of their community.

Since retiring from active clinical practice in July 2018, Dr. Morehouse has devoted himself to continued Christian growth, study, writing, and teaching about the Kingdom of God. He has had long personal and professional experience with the material covered in Celebrate Salvation.®

 His Kingdom Press
Rochester, New York 14619

Special discounts are available on quantity purchases by corporations, associations, educators, and others. For details, contact the publisher through www.hiskingdom.us/press.

Saved Contents

Acknowledgements

The work you have in your hands is part of a collaboration with roots that extend back for generations and even millennia. Jesus came to reveal God's love to struggling mankind and to demonstrate the depth of that love in ways that have had a profound impact on countless lives ever since. He embodied the fullness of God in human form and called us out of darkness, confusion, and bondage into the wonderful light, clarity, and freedom we were created to inhabit.

We appear to start out so fresh and pure as infants but soon become soiled and spoiled. Then as the years go by we get deeper and deeper in. As the Psalmist wrote:

The LORD looks down from heaven on the children of man, to see if there are any who understand, who seek after God. They have all turned aside; together they have become corrupt; there is none who does good, not even one.

Psalm 14:2-3, also noted in Psalm 53:1-3 and Romans 3:10-12

How can we come clean? Do you believe in second, third, and even seven times seventieth chances? God does.

Historically, there were entire eras when certain troubling human conditions, like addictions and criminal behavior, were just written off as hopeless. This work owes a deep debt of ongoing gratitude, first to the God who saves and then to fellow believers in the Body of Christ who are working tirelessly to reveal and share the truth that God hears our prayers and has life-giving answers for even our most challenging and "unsolvable" problems.

Many people are continuing to contribute their prayers, thoughts, ideas, and constructive comments to the growth and development of Celebrate Salvation.® I am particularly grateful for the pioneering work of John Baker, Rick Warren, and their colleagues at Saddleback Church as well as to many contributors in my local church fellowship and beyond. I would especially like to honor my wife and life partner, Susan, for her unfailing love and support over the decades we have been given to share life, faith, family, and community together.

Meeting 21ˢᵗ Century Needs

Celebrate Salvation® has developed a broad-based Christ-centered study series and discipleship program designed to reach a wide audience of sincere seekers. Are you searching for truth in our troubled age, a new believer seeking to be grounded, someone who has recently renewed your faith commitment in Christ and wants to revitalize your faith and ability to be an effective witness to others, or a church leader committed to growth? If so, this course is for you.

Celebrate Salvation's® underlying design is based on a set of several Biblical understandings first clearly outlined during the Oxford Group revival in the early 20ᵗʰ Century. One outgrowth of this movement became the time-honored 12-Steps and Traditions of Alcoholics Anonymous which have been instrumental in helping millions find God-given strength to overcome addictive behaviors. However, since then many 12-step recovery programs have revised their terminology to reach people who've had negative experiences with organized religion by replacing references to "God" with the term "a higher power" which is left up to each participant to define.

In the 1990s the 12-Step approach was significantly reframed by John Baker and Rick Warren at Saddleback Church into a clearly Christian program compatible with its Oxford Group roots. Following the original understandings, they condensed the 12 Steps of Anonymous programs back down to 8 Principles or Choices coupled with Bible references. Since then millions more have followed their highly-successful Celebrate Recovery® (CR) program to find freedom in Christ and victory over a wide array of common human difficulties.

Over the years, many have observed that Step programs capture the essential and lifelong Biblical dynamics involved in becoming a spiritually born again believer and active disciple of Jesus Christ. 12-Step programs may hold meetings in houses of worship but choose to operate independently of religion. On the other hand, CR was designed to be sponsored by local churches as an outreach ministry with a focus on people who self-identify as needing recovery from a number of challenging life situations, including addictions. In any given area there also may or may not be an active CR presence, a situation that calls for a discipleship program with a wider reach and deeper integration with the core mission of the church.

Sadly, struggles with pornography and other negative or destructive attitudes or behaviors that impair a Christian's walk with Christ are not generally covered in pulpit messages or new member classes for a number of reasons. Perhaps it's because people may be reluctant to be open about potentially embarrassing problems or individual home fellowship groups or congregations may lack the capacity to handle them. Access to Christian growth and discipleship resources for helping members and new believers overcome personal issues and become solidly rooted in their faith may also be limited.

Now in the 21st century we are again facing widespread social changes that are challenging the moral and spiritual roots of our civilization. As the prophet said,

Justice is turned back, and righteousness stands far away; for truth has stumbled in the public squares, and uprightness cannot enter.   Isaiah 59:14

Many of us find ourselves aching for an outpouring of God's Holy Spirit, for times of widespread revival and spiritual awakening. Are we prepared? What would happen if God were to answer our prayers and pour out His Spirit throughout our communities, breaking open those already in the church and bringing in a large influx of new believers laden with the issues of our modern world? Would we and our churches know how to handle an Awakening like this?

Celebrate Salvation® has taken the Oxford Group's understandings, as modified by 12-Step and CR programs, and clarified them further with grateful credit to make them available to the church at large.

Discovering the ever-unfolding mystery of faith in the living God is a wonderfully profound, life-changing, and satisfying gift. Our hope is that this modest series of introductory studies will provide a Biblically balanced and sound foundation for the faith which is widely applicable, reproducible, and fruitful. Please use the materials in *The Joy of Christian Discipleship Series* and augment them with those of your own fellowship group as we seek to meet the needs of our time with God's faithful Word.

Dr. Bill Morehouse
October 2020

Meeting 21st Century Needs

Celebrate Salvation!®

The Joy of Christian Discipleship Course 1

Established in 3 Stages and 7 Steps

Saved! Rescued by Grace

A - Foundational Principles of the Good News

1. Recognize the trouble I'm in: Admit that I'm dealing with issues that are beyond my control and need help getting and keeping my life on the right track.

2. Believe in God's love: Believe that God is really in charge, loves me, and earnestly desires to exercise His Kingdom power to rescue me and work it all out.

3. Let go and let God: Consciously choose to commit all my life and will to Jesus Christ's care and control.

Sanctified: Coming Clean with God

B - Living in the Word and the World

4. Conviction and Repentance: Evaluate my life and all my relationships in the light of the Holy Spirit and then openly confess my faults to myself, to God, and to others that I trust. Forgive those who have hurt me and seek restitution and reconciliation wherever possible.

5. Trust and Obey: Voluntarily submit to any and all changes God wants to make in my life and humbly ask Him to cleanse me and progressively remove all my character defects.

6. Communicating with God: Reserve dedicated time with God for self-examination, Bible reading, fasting and prayer in order to know God and His will for my life and to gain the power to follow His will.

Sent: Becoming a Living Letter

C - Sharing the Good News of God's Kingdom

7. The Great Commission: Celebrate the joy of my salvation by following God's lead in bringing His Good News to others in Word, Deed, and Power.

Background Material

About Course 1

The material in **Course 1** of *The Joy of Christian Discipleship Series* has been developed in the form of three books, 1-3, one for each foundational Stage of Christian discipleship with significant expansion on the Great Commission in the third. These workbooks are designed to serve as study guides for small discipleship groups of 2-10 (ideal 3-7) committed members. Each of the three studies can be completed in about 12 weekly group sessions over one semester or 3-month period with breaks for holidays.

New groups may gather and start at any time with mature leaders who have already gone through the material themselves or have been raised up in similar 12-Step and/or CR programs in other settings. A good way for congregations to get a Celebrate Salvation® course going in their church is to gather current members together who have had some experience in discipleship or recovery groups and embark on a planning process for reviewing and introducing the study series into the life of their fellowship. It's not only wise but essential to plan on organizing separate groups for men and women, given the personal nature of discipleship and the relationships that develop, including those between leaders and members newer in the faith.

Each of the three guides in **Course 1** is divided into twelve 4-page weekly lessons containing four lessons on each of the three Steps in the first two guides and four lessons on carrying out the Great Commission in Word, Deed, and Power in the third. Supplementary handouts and worksheets designed to accompany each book in the series are available in a companion book or online at www.celebratesalvation.org/more.

This first guide is entitled *Saved! Rescued by Grace* and covers what it means to be saved by God's grace and start rebuilding our lives on God's firm foundation.

"Everyone who comes to me and hears my words and does them, I will show you what he is like: he is like a man building a house, who dug deep and laid the foundation on the rock." Luke 6:47-48

... a foundation of repentance from dead works and of faith toward God, and of instruction about washings, the laying on of hands, the resurrection of the dead, and eternal judgment. Hebrews 6:1-2

Discipleship Course Design

Course 1 Group Guidelines

1. Prepare for each meeting by reading the week's lesson and writing out your answers to the questions in advance.
2. Please keep your group sharing focused on your own thoughts, feelings, experiences, and insights about each question. Limit your sharing to allow others time to share.
3. Try to avoid cross-talk. Cross-talk is when people interrupt or engage in side conversations that exclude others. Each person should be free to express their own feelings without interruptions.
4. We are here to support one another, not to instruct, preach at, or "fix" one another.
5. Anonymity and confidentiality are essential requirements in a trusting discipleship group. Personal information that is shared in the group stays in the group unless permission is given or someone threatens to injure themselves or others.
6. Offensive or demeaning language is unwelcome in any Christian fellowship group.
7. Please silence your personal electronic devices and put them away. Recording during meetings is prohibited.

Suggestions for Group Leadership

Organize separate groups for men and women to ensure safe, open sharing. Schedule regular weekly meetings to last about 90 minutes. Make sure all participants have study guides and access to handouts.

1. Gather group in a circle and open meeting on time with prayer and brief comments about group business and upcoming events.
2. Go around circle with introductions including first name, brief confession of faith, and primary issues for personal growth.
3. Continue around circle by reading 3 Stages and 7 Steps, followed by Group Guidelines and then, in unison, one of the Confessional Prayers.
4. Start each lesson by reading the introductory paragraphs around the circle and then opening with the first question.
5. Keep one-by-one sharing going around the circle within Guidelines.
6. Circulate basket for prayer requests; then recirculate so each person who submitted one can take a different one home for intercession.
7. Bring copies of next week's handouts for those who need them.
8. Close meeting on time with prayer, allowing members to linger for conversation for a while. Refreshments optional.

Background Material

Confession and Prayer

The 23rd Psalm

The LORD is my shepherd; I shall not want. He makes me lie down in green pastures. He leads me beside still waters. He restores my soul. He leads me in paths of righteousness for his name's sake. Even though I walk through the valley of the shadow of death, I will fear no evil, for you are with me; your rod and your staff, they comfort me. You prepare a table before me in the presence of my enemies; you anoint my head with oil; my cup overflows. Surely goodness and mercy shall follow me all the days of my life, and I shall dwell in the house of the LORD forever.

David

The LORD's Prayer

"Our Father in heaven, hallowed be Your Name. Your Kingdom come, Your will be done on earth as it is in heaven. Give us this day our daily bread, and forgive us our debts, as we forgive our debtors. Do not lead us into temptation, but deliver us from the evil one, for Yours is the Kingdom and the power and the glory forever. Amen."

Jesus

The Serenity Prayer

God, grant me the serenity to accept the things I cannot change, the courage to change the things I can, and the wisdom to know the difference. Living one day at a time, enjoying one moment at a time; accepting hardship as a pathway to peace; taking, as Jesus did, this sinful world as it is, not as I would have it; trusting that You will make all things right if I surrender to Your will; so that I may be reasonably happy in this life and supremely happy with You forever in the next. Amen.

Reinhold Niebuhr

Prayer

What is this all about?

O ne way to open up the subject of this entire series is to start way back with a Bible account that many of us have heard about – the story in Exodus of Moses leading the people of Israel out of slavery in Egypt, over the Red Sea, and across the wilderness of Sinai to the Promised Land of Canaan.

As you may recall, Jacob (renamed Israel) and his extended family fled during a famine to Egypt where his son Joseph had risen to authority in Pharaoh's court. For several generations they prospered until falling out of favor and becoming enslaved. After crying out for relief, God sent help and deliverance in the person of Moses who confronted Pharaoh and then called and led the Israelites out miraculously.

It happened this way: Any who would believe were instructed to sacrifice a lamb and smear its blood over the doorposts of their home so that the Death Angel would pass over their household. "Passover" was instituted as an annual celebration of salvation and rescue. The sacrifice of the lamb foreshadowed the Messiah's public bloodshed, death, and remarkable resurrection on Easter morning.

After separating from the Egyptians and miraculously crossing the divided Red Sea on dry ground the Israelites went through a prolonged period of wilderness testing. They arrived at Canaan's border purified and equipped, ready to enter in and possess the Promised Land under the leadership of Joshua.

Background Material

This historic series of events is a model of what we, Jews and Gentiles, have been invited to experience since the pivotal life, death, and resurrection of Jesus of Nazareth two millennia ago.

In this life we find ourselves ensnared and suffering in a world of humanity within and around us, a world that promised life and love but has delivered betrayal, deception, and unintended consequences mixed in with goodness. We discover that we've become slaves in Egypt, so to speak. We cry out, each in our own way, and God sends His own Son. Jesus reveals Himself to any who are ready to believe in Him and leads us in paths of deliverance and restoration to the good future of our own Promised Land, the Kingdom of God.

Was it easy for the Israelites, accustomed as they were to life as slaves in Egypt, to leave the old way, trust and follow the guidance of Moses, and undergo the changes, instruction, and personal growth brought about as they traveled through the uncharted territories of the wilderness? No. Was it easy for them to arrive at the Promised Land only to discover that they had to "take" it using the new life skills they had developed in the wilderness? No. Would it have been easier to stay back in bondage in Egypt? No!!

The process described in the Torah, which means "Teaching" or "Law" and is also known as the Pentateuch (the first five books of the Bible), was a one-way street, a difficult one to be sure but one with an outstanding guide and a very good outcome. The same is true for the path we've been called to take from our lives as slaves to sin through salvation and sanctification and on into being sent. And when it's all said and done, the rewards are literally out of this world.

Gracious is the LORD, and righteous; our God is merciful. The LORD preserves the simple; when I was brought low, he saved me. Return, O my soul, to your rest; for the LORD has dealt bountifully with you. For you have delivered my soul from death, my eyes from tears, my feet from stumbling; I will walk before the LORD in the land of the living. Psalm 116:5-9

Welcome to the journey of a lifetime!

What is this all about?

Saved! Rescued by Grace
A - Foundational principles of the Good News

But now the righteousness of God has been manifested apart from the law, although the Law and the Prophets bear witness to it – the righteousness of God through faith in Jesus Christ for all who believe. For there is no distinction: for all have sinned and fall short of the glory of God, and are justified by his grace as a gift, through the redemption that is in Christ Jesus. Romans 3:21-24

Is life really a beach?

What does it mean to be rescued? Let's go to the beach to find out. Sunshine, sand castles, cool water, good eats – this is the life!

Wait just a minute! They won't let you into the nice beach areas like all the other people who are out there having fun? They only want you to work or pick up trash? Rude people kick sand in your face and make fun of you there? The water is scary and you never learned how to swim? The last time you were out there you almost drowned? You're drowning now?? Well, life does have its problems, including mayhem and mortality and everything in between. What on earth can we do with all these issues? But we've gotten off track: we were talking about rescue.

Let's suppose you're at the beach, and you've been doing pretty well or having a hard time, it really doesn't matter. You've gone for a swim – the buoys between you and the shore say you've gone too far – and somehow you've gotten in over your head. The waves have knocked you down and now you can't breathe or get back to shore. You were either too ashamed, too distracted, or too proud to call for help sooner. Now you're overwhelmed. What do you do?

It's time to cry out for help and hope and pray that someone who knows what to do will come to your rescue, a Life Guard who cares enough to risk their own life because the waves are really strong out where you are. You're going up and down frantically as you call out, your whole life streaming before your very eyes, and the next thing you know arms stronger than yours are hauling your sputtering body back to shore.

You're out of it when you arrive, can't think straight or breathe, but the Life Guard rolls you over, clears your lungs, and revives you. Then he leaves you on the shore to take care of yourself, right? No, he goes the extra mile, dries you off and puts a warm robe on you, smiles and encourages you, forgives you for disobeying the warning signs and going out too far, gets you the help you need, pays for your beach fees, and enrolls you in a free swimming class where he is the instructor. Let me tell you, that is some Life Guard!

You thought it was the end, but now your life's been given back to you, more precious than ever. You owe this person everything. What can you possibly give in return? Yes, you'll enroll in his classes and more – now you're determined to become a life guard yourself.

What has happened to you? In simple words that sound so religious in today's world, you've been rescued, revived, redeemed, and are on the way to recovery and restoration. And even more than that, you're no longer just a visitor at the beach who's out there for your own well-being and entertainment – now you're beginning to discover the joy of what it means to get in shape and become part of the beach rescue team, a disciple of the chief Life Guard.

Yes, in some ways we can say that life truly is a beach, and that's what this study is about. How can we make sure that we're really saved and then go on to live a life worthy of the One who has saved us?

I sink in deep mire, where there is no foothold; I have come into deep waters, and the flood sweeps over me... water closed over my head; I said, "I am lost." I called on your name, O LORD... You have taken up my cause... you have redeemed my life.
Psalm 69.2 and Lamentations 3:54-58

Or, in the simple words of Pastor Tim Keller, "The gospel is this: We are more sinful and flawed in ourselves than we ever dared believe, yet at the very same time we are more loved and accepted in Jesus Christ than we ever dared hope." Recognizing our need to be "Rescued by Grace" is the most critical first step. Jesus put it this way:

"Those who are well have no need of a physician, but those who are sick. I came not to call the righteous, but sinners."
Mark 2:17

Is life really a beach?

Lesson 1A
Dealing with my issues

Step 1: Recognize the trouble I'm in: Admit that I'm dealing with issues that are beyond my control and need help getting and keeping my life on the right track.

Humbly recognize that I've become entangled in unresolved and overwhelming issues. My life has reached a turning point where I'm looking for some serious help.

Man is born to trouble as surely as sparks fly upward. Job 5:7

How did we get here, and what kind of "issues" are we talking about? Well, let's just say that life is complicated, even more than we might have thought. We try hard, but we're subjected to all kinds of challenges, choices, and influences. Sometimes we handle our lives well, and other times we've made mistakes, even some serious ones. The same is true for everybody else, so we find ourselves living as imperfect people among other imperfect people in a beautiful but imperfect world. Along the way we accumulate our share of baggage with some of its associated stress symptoms of anger, anxiety, guilt, shame, loneliness, confusion, lack of motivation, you name it. If you're wondering how this might apply to you, please check out our handout **What is Baggage?** at www.celebratesalvation.org/more.

Where does all this come from? Three primary sources: the people and world around us, the urges and desires of our own human flesh, and a whole host of thoughts, ideas, and notions that seem to come into our heads from somewhere. We just soak it up, take on our own troubles and more besides, and then influence those around us in turn.

The word "influences" literally means things that flow into us like mental and motivational water. From the troubled world around us we get peer pressure, politics, news reports, education and fads. From our own human flesh we feel urges for food, acceptance, sexual comfort, and stimulation. And from the often mysterious realm of spiritual activity we not only can find inspiration, harmony, awe, beauty, peace, wisdom, and a host of other blessings but also false hope, misguided thoughts, torment, and paths that lead us astray.

Every ointment in life seems to have flies swarming in and around it. The world has a lot of wonderful features but is contaminated with error, frustration, war, and all kinds of human disorder. Our own flesh fosters desires that often go out of bounds and get us overboard into trouble. And a multitude of thoughts enter our minds that seem reasonable at the time but prove to be snares and traps. In other words, we get "hooked" on the rewards offered along the way by that notorious triad – the world, the flesh, and the devil – and end up confused not only about how we got there but how to find the way forward and the power to change in the midst of it all.

You might appreciate reading about the temptation and fall of Adam and Eve in the Garden of Eden in Chapter 3 of the Book of Genesis. Whether you believe the story literally or not, it's a graphic illustration of mankind's three enemies at work:

> *But the serpent* [devil] *said to the woman, "You will not surely die. For God knows that when you eat of it your eyes will be opened, and you will be like God, knowing good and evil. "So when the woman saw that the tree was good for food, and that it was a delight to the eyes* [flesh], *and that the tree was to be desired to make one wise* [world], *she took of its fruit and ate, and she also gave some to her husband who was with her, and he ate.*   Genesis 3:4-6

Awakening to Need

1. Have you been having stress symptoms? What kinds of personal baggage or issues could be underlying them?

2. What areas of your life do you have the most trouble with? How successful have you been in overcoming them?

3. Do you try to comfort yourself or "take a break" in difficult times by doing things to that have become problems too?

4. Do you blame your problems on yourself, other people, your circumstances, the devil, or even on God? Does that help?

14

5. Do you know anyone whose pride gets them in trouble? How about you? Could pride be one of your personal issues?

Be thorough while you're answering each question by reviewing our handout on **What is Baggage?** at www.celebratesalvation.org/more and taking notes below as well as on additional sheets of paper. Seriously consider starting to keep a daily Journal of your insights, meditations, thoughts and prayers. And if you're good at memorizing, you might even try your hand at committing some of the Scripture passages printed in dark blue to memory.

A simple prayer:

God, please help me start seeing my issues for what they are.

Lesson 2A
How am I handling them?

Step 1: Recognize the trouble I'm in: Admit that I'm dealing with issues that are beyond my control and need help getting and keeping my life on the right track.

Face the fact that I've been misled and deceived in many ways by my own thoughts, feelings, and understandings and have been hurting and hiding from God and others while trying to work things out on my own.

There are many ways that people deal with life when their conscience gets prodded. The best way is always to deal with the issues straight up: if you've been caught by your conscience doing something out of order, it's time to come clean, change your attitude and ways, and make amends to anyone who's been hurt.

But that's not the way most people usually handle things. Try reading the Genesis 4:1-16 story of Cain and Abel as a backdrop, and then let's change to the first person, get real about it, and see if any of these common human ways of managing your conscience when it sends you a message ring true to you:

1. I minimize things and hide in denial about my actual situation, cover it up, and keep thinking that I can fix my problems on my own. I just push the snooze alarm again and carry on. I figure that sooner or later this might catch up with me, but hopefully I'll be able to fix it before then and get off scot-free.

2. I make excuses for my behavior and write it off as just human failings that we're all allowed (by whom?) to have from time to time. That's just the way life is.

3. I justify what I've done by saying to myself that I deserve to step out from time to time, take a break, reward myself, and offload my stress. Doesn't everybody have stress pop-off valves like this?

4. I blame it on God, circumstances, or what other people have done to annoy, aggravate, or provoke me like the Jets sang in Westside Story: "I'm depraved on account I'm deprived!"

Saved! Rescued by Grace

It really looks like the time is up for all my evasions and excuses. I need to deal with this mess, get some serious help, and seek the "best way" I can find going forward.

As James wrote in 1:23-24, I've been *"like a man who looks intently at his natural face in a mirror... and goes away and at once forgets what he was like."* At this point I need to note Moses' warning in Numbers 32:23 to *"be sure your sin will find you out"* and start getting serious.

Where is the way back to that "right track" I've gotten off (or never was really on)? How and where can I get the help and strength I need?

Awakening to Denial

1. Did Cain come clean when confronted with his wrongdoing? Do you see anything in this story that strikes you personally?

2. What problems have you minimized, denied, and tried to hide by lying to yourself or others and covering them up?

3. What behaviors have you consistently made excuses for, even when other people have pointed them out?

4. Do you talk yourself out of taking responsibility for your actions by justifying what you do as an earned entitlement?

5. Are there things you've done that you don't feel you can rightly blame or push off onto others?

18

6. What holds you back from taking the bull of your life by the horns and dealing with it straight up?

Be thorough while you're answering each question by taking notes below as well as on additional sheets of paper. Seriously consider starting to keep a daily Journal of your insights, meditations, thoughts and prayers.

A simple prayer:

God, please show me how I've been handling my problems.

Lesson 3A
Can I really fix myself?

Step 1: Recognize the trouble I'm in: Admit that I'm dealing with issues that are beyond my control and need help getting and keeping my life on the right track.

Confess that, even though I've been trying my hardest and doing some things right, something is very wrong with how I've been going about living life: I can't seem to solve my problems on my own. In fact, without help I will only keep making them worse, because even when I recognize that something needs to change I can't seem to change it.

I have the desire to do what is right, but not the ability to carry it out. For I do not do the good I want, but the evil I do not want is what I keep on doing.

Romans 7:18-19

We all have to deal with problems. It seems like that's why we were created with brains that think, minds that can figure things out, and language so that we can communicate and work together in problem-solving. Consider this study: where would we be if we couldn't read, study, think, ponder, discuss, and learn from it? Yes, we can address these things, but our power to control many of them is limited because they're brought on by others and the challenges of the world around us.

In addition there's another category of problems – the ones that we've caused ourselves and how we've learned to approach and handle life – that seems to evade reason by messing with motivation and our ability to cope and persevere successfully (revisit our **What is Baggage?** handout from Lesson 1A). Sometimes we can recognize and identify attitudes or behaviors like these, and often we can see what the right way to handle them should be, but then we find ourselves repeating the same fruitless approaches over and over again.

There seems to be an unseen force at work in our lives that unwittingly replays old scripts as we unconsciously revisit old, unresolved injuries and their negative effects on how we behave. We think, "I'm smart. Why can't I get over this?" As a popular saying (mistakenly attributed to Albert Einstein) goes, "The definition of insanity is doing the same thing over and over again and expecting different results." Maybe all of us are even crazier than we thought!

After just so many frustrating failures, we may find ourselves crying out as Paul did a few verses further on in the Romans 7 passage we quoted at the start of this Lesson:

> *Wretched man that I am! Who will deliver me from this body of death?*
>
> Romans 7:24

This is a situation commonly referred to as "powerlessness." Even though we often don't fully recognize them, it turns out that there are a lot of God-sized problems in living life that we just weren't designed to solve on our own apart from God's amazing grace. And actually, the longer we live the more we discover that we really can't do anything entirely on our own, completely apart from His grace. It's just that sometimes we're more aware of our need, and that's a good wake-up call to reality. The solution is to listen for His call to work with Him:

> *"Come now, let us reason together," says the* LORD: *"though your sins are like scarlet, they shall be as white as snow; though they are red like crimson, they shall become like wool."*
>
> Isaiah 1:18

Awakening to Powerlessness

1. What is the most troublesome problem that you keep dealing with over and over?

2. What are some other problems that you've dealt with, and how successful have you been in overcoming them?

3. What has helped you in the past, and what are you trying to do now?

4. Are you ready to turn over your most troublesome unsolved problem to God and earnestly seek His help to overcome it? How will you do this?

22

5. What's holding you back from turning over all the unsolved problems in your life and receiving God's ongoing help?

Be thorough while you're answering each question by taking notes below as well as on additional sheets of paper. Seriously consider keeping a daily Journal of your insights, meditations, thoughts and prayers.

A simple prayer:

God, please open my heart to receive your help in my life.

Lesson 4A
Ready to get help

Step 1: Recognize the trouble I'm in: Admit that I'm dealing with issues that are beyond my control and need help getting and keeping my life on the right track.

I'm ready to evaluate my life and get help with guidance, insight, and whatever support I need. How can I connect with the ultimate source of help that will lead me into the way, truth, and life of reality?

How can we say it? Human help is helpful, but divine help is divine. We need both working together. There is nothing shameful in recognizing that you need help. I've often wondered at the thinking of people who litter their yards with broken down cars. They must be OK with it, but are they waiting for a day when they'll figure out how to get them fixed? Why don't they find someone who can help them? It seems that might be the more sensible thing to do.

Why do we hold onto our problems and just let them keep piling up and getting worse without seeking help? It could be ignorance or pride, but maybe it's because we don't know where to go, who to ask, or how we would pay for it. A long time ago, the prophet Isaiah proclaimed that God would send an answer in the form of a person:

> *For to us a child is born, to us a son is given; and the government shall be upon his shoulder, and his name shall be called Wonderful Counselor, Mighty God, Everlasting Father, Prince of Peace.* Isaiah 9:6

Then two millennia ago in fulfillment of Isaiah's prophetic word a baby was born whose life, death, and resurrection changed the world. For those who are ready to admit that they need help, Jesus is available as the Great Physician for comfort, consultation, counsel, and treatment for any problem, anytime and anywhere, without cost or condemnation. He even makes house calls! But Jesus is a gentleman: He won't come unless we recognize the needs we have that are so woven into our human condition and ask for help.

Saved! Rescued by Grace

And as he reclined at table in his house, many tax collectors and sinners were reclining with Jesus and his disciples, for there were many who followed him. And the scribes of the Pharisees, when they saw that he was eating with sinners and tax collectors, said to his disciples, "Why does he eat with tax collectors and sinners?" And when Jesus heard it, he said to them, "Those who are well have no need of a physician, but those who are sick. I came not to call the righteous, but sinners." Matthew 9:10-13

What? The Creator and God of the Universe is available to help me personally with my life? But my problems aren't big enough to bother God with. Besides, don't I need to fix myself first to be presentable? And isn't it true that "God helps those who help themselves"?

Actually, no. God helps those who ask for help and who are then eager to cooperate with Him in working things out. And since God has infinite care and capacity, there's no problem that's too small to be "God-sized" or too large for Him to manage. As Jesus said:

"One who is faithful in a very little is also faithful in much." Luke 16:10

James, the brother of Jesus, proclaimed the truth this way:

If any of you lacks wisdom, let him ask God, who gives generously to all without reproach, and it will be given him. James 1:5

Go ahead, ask! What are you waiting for?

Awakening to Asking

1. What can you think of that might make you reluctant to ask God or others for help?

2. How much of a project do you think you are? Are you in a little trouble that will pass on its own or are you ready for help?

3. What are some of your ideas about what genuine help would look or feel like? Who has helped you in the past and how?

4. Who have you or can you ask for ongoing guidance and help?

5. How would you describe your prayer life? a) absent, b) crisis mode only, c) coming around, or d) pretty active. Explain.

Be thorough while you're answering each question by taking notes below as well as on additional sheets of paper. Seriously consider keeping a daily Journal of your insights, meditations, thoughts and prayers.

A simple prayer:

O God, please help me overcome my resistance to asking for the help I need and give me the grace to receive it.

Lesson 5A
God knows and cares

Step 2: Believe in God's love: Believe that God is really in charge, loves me, and earnestly desires to exercise His amazing Grace to rescue me and work it all out.

God is all around, knows all, sees all, is ready and able to forgive and help me move forward.

When you were a child you may have heard the song "He's got the whole world in His hands" and felt your heart warmed as you and others sang it. There's something very real about child-like faith that touches God's heart of love and knits it to ours. Believing in the God of the universe is a life-changing awareness of reality that is infinitely worth seeking for, asking for, and receiving when it comes.

The God we speak of is the triune God of the Bible who is manifested in the mystery of three united Persons: Father, Son, and Holy Spirit. We come to understand that the Father revealed His love to us by sending His Son, Jesus, as a baby born of Mary, with the express purpose of reconciling us to God the Father by offering himself as a sacrifice for our sin. Jesus then, after being raised from the dead, asked the Father to send the third person of the Trinity, the Holy Spirit, to be with us as a comforter, guide, and divine source of power.

The following verses will help you in your search, but it is God Himself who will kindle hope and reveal the truth about who He is and His love for you in ways that mere words can't adequately describe. Use this lesson time to seek and find Him anew.

But to all who did receive him, who believed in his name, he gave the right to become children of God, who were born, not of blood nor of the will of the flesh nor of the will of man, but of God. John 1:12-13

For God so loved the world, that he gave his only Son, that whoever believes in him should not perish but have eternal life. John 3:16

Saved! Rescued by Grace

28

[Jesus said] *"Our Father in heaven, hallowed be your name…"*

Matthew 6:7-9

O LORD, you have searched me and known me! You know when I sit down and when I rise up; you discern my thoughts from afar. You search out my path and my lying down and are acquainted with all my ways.

Psalm 139:1-3

The LORD appeared to us in the past, saying: "I have loved you with an everlasting love; I have drawn you with unfailing kindness.

Jeremiah 31.3 (NIV)

Love is from God, and whoever loves has been born of God and knows God. Anyone who does not love does not know God, because God is love.

1 John 4:7-8

[Jesus] holds his priesthood permanently, because he continues forever. Consequently, he is able to save to the uttermost those who draw near to God through him, since he always lives to make intercession for them.

Hebrews 7:24-25

For I consider that the sufferings of this present time are not worth comparing with the glory that is to be revealed to us. For the creation waits with eager longing for the revealing of the sons of God… What then shall we say to these things? If God is for us, who can be against us? He who did not spare his own Son but gave him up for us all, how will he not also with him graciously give us all things?

Romans 8:18-19, 31-32

Believing in God's Love

1. Can you recall the first time you were aware of God's love? How did you respond then?

2. How do you imagine the God of the universe being manifest in three Persons? What does the Trinity mean to you?

3. How do you envision God now? What is His character? What might He think of you?

4. Can you see ways that God has been moving in your life? How can you improve your connection with Him?

5. Are you ready to ask God for help? What would you like help with and how would you go about asking?

Be thorough while you're answering each question by taking notes below as well as on additional sheets of paper. Become seriously committed to having a dedicated time daily for prayer, meditation, and journaling your insights and thoughts. Begin to plan for adding a regular Bible study component, too. You can find helpful handouts like **Reset Daily Prayer Guide** and **How to Start Reading the Bible** online at www.celebratesalvation.org/more to guide you in setting up your devotional time and organizing your Bible study routine.

A simple prayer:

O God, please help me believe and learn to trust in your love for me.

Lesson 6A
I believe so I can see

Step 2: Believe in God's love: Believe that God is really in charge, loves me, and earnestly desires to exercise His amazing Grace to rescue me and work it all out.

Believe in God's existence in order to experience his presence.

Now faith is the assurance of things hoped for, the conviction of things not seen. For by it the people of old received their commendation. By faith we understand that the universe was created by the word of God, so that what is seen was not made out of things that are visible... And without faith it is impossible to please him, for whoever would draw near to God must believe that he exists and that he rewards those who seek him. Hebrews 11:1-2, 6

Just think about it. Where do we actually see and believe things? Our eyes and other sense organs send information into our brains which gets met by thoughts and interpretations, and then we visualize something with the part of our mind that imagines things. Just as visual cues do, sounds and smells, tastes and textures, and even hopes and dreams can trigger images in our minds about what something or someone is like.

Let's suppose you were born without eyesight. What would your family look like to you? Let's suppose further that all you had to go on was things other people who had known your family had written about them, perhaps with a few drawings and stories. They gave you examples of how caring your family was and told you how much they really loved you. Would you believe them?

That's the kind of external witnesses we have about God and His love for us. We're told all about God on the well-established authority of the Biblical record, including the remarkable fact that we were created in His Image. We've heard and read about Jesus, the miracles he performed and teaching he did, and his claim to be the very Son of God, sent by his Father to reveal the character and nature of God in his own person.

Saved! Rescued by Grace

Augmenting this written witness we have all the reports of men and women over the centuries right up until now who have known Jesus as their Savior and can testify about the real presence of God in their lives. But even beyond this *"cloud of witnesses"* we have another, much more personal witness, which is the inner confirmation that God's own Spirit makes within us when we seek Him honestly and earnestly. It's this witness that clinches the deal.

We hear and then hope, then believe, and then *"taste and see"* (Psalm 34:8) that God is real, that He created us and loves us unconditionally, and that His promises are true. The more we learn and believe, the more we begin to lean into Him, to put more and more trust in Him. And finally we develop a solid faith in Him, a faith that can change lives and "move mountains." This is what we mean by Christian faith.

How does God reward our seeking? First He rewards us by revealing Himself and making His Word come alive to us. Then He opens our hearts to receive His full forgiveness. And then He confirms that we will find an abundant new life in Christ, a different life here and now in the midst of the world we live in, and eternal life with Him in Heaven.

What does He ask us to do in return? Just receive and trust the assurances and promises proclaimed in His Word, believe in Him, allow Him to adopt us as members of His own family, and then learn from Him how to walk it out in real time. This is truly Good News!

Believing in God's Presence

1. Does imagining Jesus as a full representation of God the Father help you relate to God personally?

2. Believing in someone involves both mental assent and a level of trust. How would you describe your current belief in God?

3. Can you think of any times when you believed in someone and then they let you down? How about your own father, for example?

4. Have you ever tried to entrust something to God and felt that your prayers weren't answered or your trust was abused?

34

5. What kind of authority or inner witness are you beginning to rest your hope on that God is really there for you now?

Be thorough while you're answering each question by taking notes below as well as on additional sheets of paper. Become seriously committed to having a dedicated time daily for prayer, meditation, and journaling your insights and thoughts. Work on setting up a daily devotional/Bible study time using our helpful handouts like **A Daily Bible Reading Plan** and **Daily Light Devotional Review** available online at www.celebratesalvation.org/more.

A simple prayer:

O God, please open the eyes of my heart to see you as you really are.

Lesson 7A
A new kind of life

Step 2: Believe in God's love: Believe that God is really in charge, loves me, and earnestly desires to exercise His amazing Grace to rescue me and work it all out.

God has and freely gives His eternal (everlasting) life, now and forever, in this life and the next.

What on earth is a new kind of life? I've already got life, and even though it's messed up, I've grown rather attached to it. Hmm…

> [Jesus] *told them a parable: "No one tears a piece from a new garment and puts it on an old garment. If he does, he will tear the new, and the piece from the new will not match the old. And no one puts new wine into old wineskins. If he does, the new wine will burst the skins and it will be spilled, and the skins will be destroyed. But new wine must be put into fresh wineskins. And no one after drinking old wine desires new, for he says, 'The old is good.'"*
>
> Luke 5:36-39

Somehow we have to get tired enough of our old ways of doing things to be ready for new life. We also have to trust the source of the new life, which raises another question: who gave you the life you have now? And who messed it up? This changes our question to one of whether we are ready to trust the One who gave us our first life (the life we've messed up) to give us a fresh start and help us build a better life, one that will last for eternity. Now that's a better take on reality!

Let's take a closer look at what the "new wine" promises to be like before we decide that the "old wine" is good enough for us.

> *For God so loved the world, that he gave his only Son, that whoever believes in him should not perish but have eternal life.*
> John 3:16

> *"I came that they may have life and have it abundantly."*
> John 10:10

> *"I will never leave you nor forsake you."*
> Hebrews 13:5

Saved! Rescued by Grace

From these three verses we find that the nourishing new life or "wine" we're promised will be *eternal* and *abundant* and come through a relationship with continuous access to God. Right now what we have is mortal, limited, and oddly estranged from God.

It looks like there isn't a choice to have both the old and the new "operating systems" running at the same time: we'll need to trade in our current life to get the promised new version. Where do we go and what do we need to do to arrange the trade-in?

> *"Ask, and it will be given to you; seek, and you will find; knock, and it will be opened to you. For everyone who asks receives, and the one who seeks finds, and to the one who knocks it will be opened. Or which one of you, if his son asks him for bread, will give him a stone? Or if he asks for a fish, will give him a serpent? If you then, who are evil, know how to give good gifts to your children, how much more will your Father who is in heaven give good things to those who ask him!"*

Matthew 7:7-11

Ah! Look at that! Another promise, this time that what God has in store for us is *good things* with Him that will last beyond this life into the next. As long as I can trust in His judgment about how to handle the transition, this is starting to sound like very Good News indeed.

Believing in God and His Promises

1. Can you think of any times when you've waited for a promise to be kept and ended up disappointed? What were the problems?

2. Have you ever thought that God had promised you something but didn't deliver? What happened?

3. What kind of hopes and dreams does God's promise of eternal life bring to your mind?

4. What parts of your life would you like to see infused with God's abundant life?

5. If you could talk with God person-to-person any time you wanted
    to (and you can!), what are some of the questions you would ask?
    Write them down and then review them later.

Be thorough while you're answering each question by taking extra notes
below as well as on additional sheets of paper as needed. You may
appreciate reading our handout entitled **What is Salvation All About?**
(available online at www.celebratesalvation.org/more) for more insight
into this week's topic.

A simple prayer:

O God, please help me receive and believe in You and Your promises.

Lesson 8A
The door of forgiveness

Step 2: Believe in God's love: Believe that God is really in charge, loves me, and earnestly desires to exercise His amazing Grace to rescue me and work it all out.

Learn about and understand the free gift of forgiveness that allows me to pass from death and eternal judgment to resurrection life through the shed blood of Jesus on my behalf.

What do we do when we make mistakes?

If we recognize that our errors have had a negative effect on others, there's a time-honored approach to handling the situation: reach out to those who've been offended with a humble apology and seek forgiveness, payment for losses, and reconciliation. But what if the primary damage is more vague or to yourself? Who do you seek to reconcile with then, and what about the damage that's been done?

As unbelievable as it may seem, our infinite, all-knowing God keeps an account of everything that happens in His universe and knows the damage every error has done, large or small. In this regard, we can say that ultimately the errors we make, intentionally and unintentionally, accumulate to the Creator's account. As David, the Psalmist confessed:

Against you, you only, have I sinned and done what is evil in your sight, so that you may be justified in your words and blameless in your judgment.

Psalm 51:4

Mercifully, He is ready to receive our account, reconcile it with us, and help us recover and make whatever amends are appropriate. He even sends the Holy Spirit to convict us of our sin and turn our hearts to Him for forgiveness and reconciliation. Without His Grace we have no hope: our sins and their negative effects just keep accumulating the older we get and cause a growing breach in our relationship with those around us and our Maker.

Saved! Rescued by Grace

Behold, the LORD's hand is not shortened, that it cannot save, or his ear dull, that it cannot hear; but your iniquities have made a separation between you and your God, and your sins have hidden his face from you so that he does not hear.

Isaiah 59:1

Into this gaping separation, and in keeping with many promises in His Word, God sent a divine ambassador of reconciliation, His only begotten Son. Jesus came to demonstrate His Father's love and mercy in word, deed, and power and to reveal His eternal Kingdom. He opened the door of forgiveness into the love of God through His life, death on the cross, and unstoppable resurrection.

Jesus said to him, "I am the way, and the truth, and the life. No one comes to the Father except through me... I am the door. If anyone enters by me, he will be saved and will go in and out and find pasture." John 14:6, 10:7

To as many of us as would receive Him, Jesus became our Door of Hope into new life in the Kingdom of God where our consciences aren't covered and excused but actually forgiven and cleared.

Believing in God's Forgiveness

1. How many mistakes do you think you've accumulated in life so far? How many recently? Today?

2. Do you have places of unforgiven guilt, shame, and sin that haven't been dealt with? List some of them.

3. Are you holding any unforgiveness, resentments, grudges, or ill-will toward people who have hurt you in the past?

4. What is your understanding of why Jesus was crucified and what that has to do with your life today?

5. Ponder going through the Door of Hope to exchange your sinful life for the free gift of eternal life in Christ. Are you ready?

Be thorough while you're answering each question by taking notes below as well as on additional sheets of paper. Become seriously committed to keeping your dedicated time daily for prayer, meditation, and journaling your insights and thoughts. Continue to grow in your dedication to having a regular daily time of devotions and Bible study. You might enjoy the encouragement and insights Ann Voskamp offers in her *One Thousand Gifts Devotional* listed on Page 60.

A simple prayer:

O God, please help me seek, receive, and believe in your forgiveness.

Lesson 9A
Letting go of control and denial

Step 3: Let go and let God: Consciously choose to commit all my life and will to Jesus Christ's care and control.

Let go of my own control and denial, stop trying to handle my life on my own, and learn to hear from and trust in God more and more.

In the Book of Revelation, the apostle John recorded a very generous offer that Jesus made having to do with another door of hope:

"Behold, I stand at the door and knock. If anyone hears my voice and opens the door, I will come in to him and eat with him, and he with me."

Revelation 3:20

The Door we spoke of in Lesson 8 was Jesus himself, the Door that leads from us to His Father in heaven. In this instance the door being referred to is the door of our own hearts. Jesus says He's right outside our door, knocking and seeking entrance to come in and share with us. Will we exercise hospitality and let Him in?

Of course when we let Jesus in, we're letting the God of the universe in and there's no more hiding. He knows everything already, even though we can pretend it's hidden from Him inside our hearts as long as we keep Him out. So the question Jesus asked can be rephrased this way: Are you ready to let go of the fantasy of your denial and trust Me to come in as your Friend and your way to forgiveness, reconciliation, and new life? Will you let me be your Savior and LORD?

Now that is a serious offer, especially the second part. To say that someone is your LORD means that they're in charge:

"Why do you call me 'LORD, LORD,' and not do what I tell you?"

Luke 6:46

Saved! Rescued by Grace

44

Let's look at this a little closer. When you were in charge and calling all the shots, how many mistakes did you make? If the divine person of Jesus, incapable of making any mistakes, were in charge what would your future be like if you were yielded to His leadership?

Maybe you could pick and choose. That's as simple as Will Roger's wisdom for beating the stock market: "Just buy when they're at the bottom and sell when they're at the top." Just let Him be LORD when you need His wisdom and then make your own mind up about the rest. Huh? Not a very workable plan, on second look. How about this one?

Trust in the LORD with all your heart, and do not lean on your own understanding. In all your ways acknowledge him, and he will make straight your paths.
Proverbs 3:5-6

But what about all those things I like to do to handle stress and let off steam? I know they're probably not the best, but doesn't everyone need a break from being good from time to time? There's a better way to handle stress that brings joy and freedom:

"Come to me, all who labor and are heavy laden, and I will give you rest. Take my yoke upon you, and learn from me, for I am gentle and lowly in heart, and you will find rest for your souls. For my yoke is easy, and my burden is light."
Matthew 11:28-30

Letting Go

1. Denial is a fruitless form of self-defense. What do you think you've been trying to hide from God and even from yourself?

2. When Jesus knocked at your door did you let Him in? If so, what did He say when you talked with Him?

3. If life were all bad, it might seem easier to let go. What do you think you're ready to let go of now?

4. How do you feel about asking Jesus not only to rescue you from your current problems but to take control of your life?

5. Do you think it's possible to get rescued without letting go? Or by only asking God to be your copilot in the second seat?

Be thorough while you're answering each question by taking notes below as well as on additional sheets of paper. Review and refresh your commitment to maintaining a dedicated time daily for Bible study, prayer, meditation, and journaling your insights and thoughts.

A simple prayer:

O God, please help me see and let go of my denial and urge to control!

Step 3   Lesson 9A

Lesson 10A
You must be born again

Step 3: Let go and let God: Consciously choose to commit all my life and will to Jesus Christ's care and control.

Give my life to Jesus and be born spiritually from above ("born again") to be united with Him, receive His everlasting life now, and be adopted into His forever family.

Now we get to the place where, as auto racers say, the rubber hits the road. Or, as fishermen say, we have to choose whether we're going to fish or cut bait. Are we just going to pretend by talking the talk or are we ready to walk the walk?

To put things plainly, you can't ask Jesus to be your Savior without accepting Him as your Lord at the same time. You're starting over, and it's no longer your life to do with as you please, it's His. You've been bought back (the religious/pawnbroker's word is "redeemed") by the very one who created you, and now you're His. Believe me when I say that being redeemed by Jesus Christ is Good News that gets better and better.

For by grace you have been saved through faith. And this is not your own doing; it is the gift of God, not a result of works, so that no one may boast.

Ephesians 2:8-9

The terminology Jesus used was that salvation involves being born again from above and starting over spiritually as an adopted child of your Heavenly Father.

Nicodemus, a ruler of the Jews… came to Jesus by night and said to him, "Rabbi, we know that you are a teacher come from God, for no one can do these signs that you do unless God is with him." Jesus answered him, "Truly, truly, I say to you, unless one is born again he cannot see the kingdom of God." Nicodemus said to him, "How can a man be born when he is old? Can he enter a second time into his mother's womb and be born?" Jesus answered, "Truly, truly, I say to you, unless one is born of water and the Spirit, he cannot enter the kingdom of God."

John 3:1-4

Saved! Rescued by Grace

Born again simply means that as newborn babies just starting out need nurture, love, training, guidance, and being raised up into maturity, our spiritual lives also need a clear starting point of conviction, repentance, commitment, and discipleship.

"Truly, I say to you, unless you turn and become like children, you will never enter the kingdom of heaven."
Matthew 18:3

As you learn to walk as a newborn Christian, sometimes you're going to make some mistakes and even fall. But rest assured that God will be there to pick you up, comfort, and encourage you. What's called for on our part is seeking, asking, listening, and following. He leads us into our new life in His Kingdom, and we learn to trust in Him and obey.

"Therefore do not be anxious, saying, 'What shall we eat?' or 'What shall we drink?' or 'What shall we wear?' For… your heavenly Father knows that you need them all. But seek first the kingdom of God and his righteousness, and all these things will be added to you."
Matthew 6:31-33

It sounds pretty easy, and it actually is once you start getting used to it. But every life and every journey has to start somewhere, and the new life that God has prepared for His people starts with being born again, waking up and breathing the pure air of His Holy Spirit.

Letting Go

1. Is anything holding you back from letting go completely and letting God take charge of your life?

2. Do you like babies and children? What it would be like to have a perfect father and a loving family to grow up in?

3. Children often have trouble becoming fully adopted because they can't let go of old attachments. Could this affect you?

4. What experiences, ideas, or questions do you have about being born again? Who can you talk with about this?

50

5. Are you ready? Can God be trusted and taken at His Word? Is
    anything holding you back?

Be thorough while you're answering each question by taking notes on
additional sheets of paper. Review and refresh your commitment to
maintaining a dedicated time daily for Bible study, prayer, meditation,
and journaling your insights and thoughts.

*Out of my distress I called on the Lord; the Lord answered me and set
me free… O give thanks to the Lord, for he is good; for his steadfast love
endures forever!*
                                                    Psalm 118:5, 29

A prayer to be born again

*Dear God, I want to be forgiven and adopted into your family. You said in
Your Word that if I acknowledge that you raised Jesus from the dead and receive
Him as my Lord and Savior, I would be saved. Heavenly Father, I now confess
that I believe you raised Jesus from the dead and that He is alive and well. I
accept Him now as my personal Lord and Savior. I receive your offer to forgive
me, adopt me into your family, and raise me up in newness of life.*

Lesson 11A
Being baptized in water

Step 3: Let go and let God: Consciously choose to commit all my life and will to Jesus Christ's care and control.

Publicly let go of our old self-directed life to embrace God's free gift of eternal life by receiving (or reaffirming) baptism in water by immersion.

Then Jesus came from Galilee to the Jordan to John, to be baptized by him. John would have prevented him, saying, "I need to be baptized by you, and do you come to me?" But Jesus answered him, "Let it be so now, for thus it is fitting for us to fulfill all righteousness." Then he consented. And when Jesus was baptized, immediately he went up from the water, and behold, the heavens were opened to him, and he saw the Spirit of God descending like a dove and coming to rest on him; and behold, a voice from heaven said, "This is my beloved Son with whom I am well pleased." Matthew 3:13-17

Peter replied, "Repent and be baptized, every one of you, in the name of Jesus Christ for the forgiveness of your sins. And you will receive the gift of the Holy Spirit." Acts 2:38

We were buried therefore with him by baptism into death, in order that, just as Christ was raised from the dead by the glory of the Father, we too might walk in newness of life. Romans 6:4

Just what is this "baptism" that the Scriptures talk about? It's helpful to understand that our English word "baptize" is simply a transliteration of the Biblical Greek word βαπτίζω (*baptizo*), which means to immerse completely in a fluid like water. If it were translated directly, our word would be "immerse" (or "whelm" which we easily recognize in the compound word "overwhelmed" or drowning). In contrast, we often say we are "underwhelmed" if the experience is too shallow. We get "whelmed" when we dive right in and enjoy the swim.

In the early centuries of the faith, it was widely understood that being baptized by immersion (also known as *credobaptism*) was something that

52

happened after a person understood the Gospel message, repented, and received Christ as their LORD and Savior. It was then, and remains now, a public confirmation of faith, a mature turning point.

The practice of "baptizing" infants and children (also known as *pedobaptism*) began in times when child mortality rates were high and parents were concerned that their children might die without the opportunity of reaching heaven (see 1 Corinthians 7:14 and Acts 2:38-39 for reassurance). Perhaps for safety's sake, the babies were sprinkled with water instead of being immersed.

After Constantine adopted Christianity as the official religion of the Roman Empire people wanted to assure that every member of their family would be counted as a full citizen in the Empire. Pedobaptism was likened by the Roman Church to the Old Testament covenant of circumcision and eventually took the place of immersion baptism based on confession of faith throughout much of organized Christendom.

Wherever the need for believers to enter into Christian faith through new birth has been recognized, however, the reality that infant dedication does not replace Biblical adult baptism has been noted. Every new believer must decide whether they have been obedient to the Scriptural mandate that baptism signifies.

Letting God

1. What do you know about any ceremonies of dedication or infant "baptism" that may have happened to you as a child?

2. Have you been baptized after becoming a believer in a way that makes Biblical sense to you?

3. Would you like to be baptized? What areas of your flesh do you want to leave behind in the waters of baptism?

4. What would the process and consequences be for you if you were baptized by immersion? What would your family think?

54

5. Do you have any unanswered questions about this topic? Where will you go to seek answers?

We have a handout called **Essentials of Water Baptism** available online at www.celebratesalvation.org/more that you may find helpful.

A prayer for the blessings of water baptism

Heavenly Father, I thank you for calling me to be baptized in water as a sign of the death of my old self-directed life, and the resurrection of the new person that you are making me with Christ Jesus as my Lord and Savior. Please allow my old self to be buried as it goes under the waters in baptism, and my new self to come alive as I come up out of the waters as the new person you want me to be.

As you prepare to move on to the last lesson in our study guide, you might enjoy reading about Jesus healing a blind man in Mark 8:22-26:

They came to Bethsaida, and some people brought a blind man and begged Jesus to touch him. He took the blind man by the hand and led him outside the village. When he had spit on the man's eyes and put his hands on him, Jesus asked, "Do you see anything?" He looked up and said, "I see people; they look like trees walking around." Once more Jesus put his hands on the man's eyes. Then his eyes were opened, his sight was restored, and he saw everything clearly.

Many people over the centuries have wondered why Jesus needed to lay hands on the man's eyes twice before he received his full sight. The Venerable Bede (c. 700 AD) offered the following explanation: "By this miracle, Christ teaches us how great is the spiritual blindness of man, which only by degrees, and by successive stages, can come to the light of Divine knowledge." Perhaps we all need at least two touches…

Lesson 12A
Receiving the Holy Spirit

Step 3: Let go and let God: Consciously choose to commit all my life and will to Jesus Christ's care and control.

Learn about, understand, and enter into God's power to lead a new life by receiving (or reaffirming) baptism in the Holy Spirit, often with the laying on of hands.

Since the word "baptism" means to immerse, what could the "baptism in the Holy Spirt" mean other than to be immersed in the Holy Spirit? Let's look at a couple images. If the Holy Spirit is visualized as the fluid in a pitcher, which of the following most represents what baptism in this fluid would look like?

Immersed in the Holy Spirit

Inside and Out

Holy Spirit Poured in from Outside

Separate Pitcher

Actually, the Holy Spirit isn't in a separate faraway place but is present and active all around us. As Acts 17:28 points out, *In Him we live and move and have our being.* The Spirit is ever-present sustaining the universe in order, sharing God the Father's "common" grace of Love and Wisdom, convicting us of our sin and His righteousness, and leading us to His Son for salvation.

Once the grace of the Holy Spirit has illuminated our hearts we can see our true situation and turn from our sin to receive Jesus as our LORD and Savior. The process of becoming a new believer has begun. We then need to receive God's full power for the new life we've been given to be fruitful, to stop relying on our own strength as our power source and open ourselves up to God's power. Water baptism confirms our decision

Saved! Rescued by Grace

56

and sets us on a new road in life. In Holy Spirit baptism we invite the fullness of His Holy Spirit to flow into us. This is how Jesus did it at the start of His earthly ministry:

Now when all the people were baptized, and when Jesus also had been baptized and was praying, the heavens were opened, and the Holy Spirit descended on him.
Luke 3:21-22

The Book of Acts opens with an account of Jesus' words after his resurrection and appearance to the Apostles:

He ordered them not to depart from Jerusalem, but to wait for the promise of the Father, which, he said, "you heard from me; for John baptized with water, but you will be baptized with the Holy Spirit not many days from now."
Acts 1:4-5

After coming to faith (belief) in Jesus and turning (repentance) from dead works we are offered two baptisms, one in water (confirmation) and the other in the Holy Spirit (empowerment). These may come in either order but both are facilitated by seeking, asking, and joining in prayer, often with the laying on of hands.

Peter and John... came down and prayed for them that they might receive the Holy Spirit, for He had not yet fallen on any of them, but they had only been baptized in the name of the LORD Jesus. Then they laid their hands on them and they received the Holy Spirit.
Acts 8:14-17

Letting God

1. Have you earnestly sought in prayer to be baptized in the Holy Spirit, possibly through the laying on of hands?

2. If so, what has your experience been? Have you received any of the gifts of the Holy Spirit described in 1 Corinthians 12-14?

3. If not, what concerns do you have about taking this step? Who could you talk with to work through your concerns?

4. 1 Corinthians 12 lists varieties of ways the Spirit may work in us for the common good. Which ones are you drawn to?

5. Galatians 5:22-23 describes the fruit that believers empowered by the Holy Spirit have. Would you like to be fruitful like this?

As you consider prayer to receive the fullness of the Holy Spirit you may wish to read our handout called **The Ministry of the Holy Spirit** and then follow up with **Gifts and Life in the Holy Spirit** discussing the baptism, both posted online at www.celebratesalvation.org/more.

A prayer to be baptized in the Holy Spirit

Heavenly Father, I come to you with a grateful heart for sending Jesus to save me. I pray that you would send your Holy Spirit to surround and fill me. I open my heart to receive the baptism in the Holy Spirit from you right now by faith in Your Word. May the anointing, the glory, and the power of God come upon me and into my life right now. May I be empowered for service from this day forward. Thank You, Father, for baptizing me in Your Holy Spirit, in Jesus' name. Amen.

This is a good topic to close our first study with, since the comfort, encouragement, gifts, power, presence, wisdom, and fruit of the Holy Spirit are the very milk and meat of discipleship. Between now and the start of the second guide in our course, try to do a solid Bible study of the Holy Spirit. If you haven't already, please remember to keep up your commitment to having a dedicated time daily for Bible study, prayer, meditation, and journaling your insights and thoughts. You can never get too much!

Commendation

Congratulations! You've just completed our study of what it is to face your life straight up and be rescued by Jesus from the snares of not only your own mistakes but from the negative influences of others and the fallen world we live in. We've taken Him up on his offer to be the LORD of our lives by being set apart through baptism and empowered by the Holy Spirit to live a new life for Him in this world.

May we shout for joy over your salvation, and in the name of our God set up our banners! Psalms 20:5

Now what? The following anecdote may provide a foretaste:

Billy Graham was once asked, "If Christianity is valid, why is there so much evil in the world?" To this the famous preacher replied, "With so much soap, why are there so many dirty people in the world? Christianity, like soap, must be personally applied if it is to make a difference in our lives."

Our next study guide, *Sanctified: Coming Clean with God*, will help you grow in faith as the LORD invites you to cooperate with His Word and Spirit while He continues an ongoing work of cleansing and establishment in your life that human effort could never do.

Let's keep it up together with Him as we investigate what is involved not only in making your life whole but keeping it that way by purifying and enriching it so that you can live and bear fruit in every good work.

May our LORD and Savior continue to bless, favor, encourage, and sanctify you for service in His Kingdom!

But God, being rich in mercy, because of the great love with which he loved us, even when we were dead in our trespasses, made us alive together with Christ – by grace you have been saved – and raised us up with him and seated us with him in the heavenly places in Christ Jesus. Ephesians 2:4-6

Suggestions for Further Study

The Holy Bible
English Standard Version® ESV Study Bible™.

Samuel Bagster family
Daily Light on the Daily Path. Morning evening Bible devotions.

James Choung
True Story: A Christianity Worth Believing In.

E. Stanley Jones
The Kingdom of God: Is it Realism?

C. S. Lewis
Mere Christianity.

J. I. Packer
Knowing God.

Derek Prince
The Foundation Series in a set of 7 booklets.

A. J. Russell
For Sinners Only.

Bob Sorge
Reset: 20 Ways to a Consistent Prayer Life.

Ann Voskamp
One Thousand Gifts Devotional and *The Broken Way.*

Dallas Willard
The Spirit of the Disciplines: Understanding How God Changes Lives.

Notes and References

Additional Celebrate Salvation® Resources

Books in the Joy of Christian Discipleship Series

The Joy of Christian Discipleship Course 1
Established in 3 Stages and 7 Steps, a 36-week group study

1. A - Saved! *Rescued by Grace* (this book)

    Saved Handouts *
      Group Leadership Suggestions
      What is Baggage? (1A)
      Reset Daily Prayer Guide (5A)
      How to Start Reading the Bible (5A)
      A Daily Bible Reading Plan (6A)
      Daily Light Devotional Review (6A)
      What is Salvation All About? (7A)
      Essentials of Water Baptism (11A)
      Holy Spirit Ministry *and* Gifts and Life (12A)

2. **B - Sanctified:** *Coming Clean with God*

3. **C - Sent:** *Becoming a Living Letter*

    Plus - Handouts and Worksheets *or* **Complete Course 1**

An 8-week Devotional Guide to 3 Stages and 7 Steps
4. **Essentials of the Christian Faith:**
    7 Steps to Abundant Life, an 8-week daily devotional guide

The Joy of Christian Discipleship Course 2
Equipped in 3 Realms with 7 Understandings, a 36-week group
study for Christians who are established in their faith

5. **D - Awakening:** *The Triumph of Truth*

6. **E - Kingdom:** *God's Reign in our Midst*

7. **F - Heaven:** *Our Ultimate Destiny*

    Plus - Handouts and Worksheets *or* **Complete Course 2**

The Biblical Festivals, including A Passover Seder
An illuminating introduction to God's "appointed times"

*Links to all Handouts in printable PDF form as well as Additional
Resources can be found online at www.celebratesalvation.org/more.

Saved! Rescued by Grace

62

Notes and References